50 Busy Parent Recipes for Home

By: Kelly Johnson

Table of Contents

- One-Pot Chicken Alfredo
- Sheet Pan Fajitas
- Slow Cooker Chili
- Easy Beef Stir-Fry
- Veggie-loaded Spaghetti Bolognese
- Instant Pot Chicken and Rice
- Baked Parmesan Crusted Salmon
- Turkey and Vegetable Skillet
- Quinoa Stuffed Bell Peppers
- BBQ Pulled Pork Sandwiches
- Creamy Tomato Basil Soup
- Mediterranean Chicken Wraps
- Teriyaki Tofu Stir-Fry
- Sausage and Peppers Pasta
- Honey Garlic Shrimp Stir-Fry
- Cheesy Broccoli and Rice Casserole
- Greek Salad with Grilled Chicken
- Beef and Vegetable Kebabs
- Lemon Garlic Tilapia
- Vegetarian Black Bean Tacos
- Pesto Pasta with Cherry Tomatoes
- Buffalo Chicken Lettuce Wraps
- Spinach and Ricotta Stuffed Shells
- Cajun Shrimp and Sausage Skillet
- Coconut Curry Chicken
- Caprese Quinoa Salad
- Beef and Broccoli Stir-Fry
- Hawaiian BBQ Chicken Pizza
- Creamy Mushroom Risotto
- Turkey Meatball Subs
- Lentil Soup with Spinach
- Margherita Flatbread Pizza
- Sweet and Sour Tofu
- Chicken and Vegetable Quesadillas
- Garlic Butter Shrimp Pasta

- Mediterranean Veggie Bowls
- Spicy Sausage and Pepper Pasta
- Orange Glazed Salmon
- Ratatouille
- BBQ Chicken Stuffed Sweet Potatoes
- Veggie Fried Rice
- Creamy Tuscan Chicken
- Mexican Street Corn Salad
- Beef and Mushroom Stroganoff
- Chickpea Curry
- Caprese Chicken Skillet
- Butternut Squash Soup
- Thai Basil Beef Stir-Fry
- Spinach and Feta Turkey Burgers
- Lemon Herb Grilled Chicken

One-Pot Chicken Alfredo

Ingredients:

- 1 lb (450g) boneless, skinless chicken breasts, cut into bite-sized pieces
- 8 oz (225g) fettuccine pasta
- 2 tablespoons olive oil
- 2 cloves garlic, minced
- 2 cups (480ml) chicken broth
- 1 cup (240ml) heavy cream
- 1 cup (100g) grated Parmesan cheese
- Salt and black pepper to taste
- Chopped fresh parsley for garnish (optional)

Instructions:

In a large skillet or pot, heat the olive oil over medium heat. Add the minced garlic and cook for about 1 minute until fragrant.

Add the chicken pieces to the skillet and season with salt and pepper. Cook until the chicken is browned on all sides and cooked through, about 5-7 minutes. Remove the chicken from the skillet and set aside.

In the same skillet, add the chicken broth and fettuccine pasta. Bring to a boil, then reduce the heat to medium-low and simmer, stirring occasionally, until the pasta is cooked and most of the liquid has been absorbed, about 10-12 minutes.

Stir in the heavy cream and grated Parmesan cheese until the cheese is melted and the sauce is creamy.

Add the cooked chicken back to the skillet and stir to combine with the sauce and pasta.

Taste and adjust the seasoning with salt and pepper if needed.

Serve the one-pot chicken Alfredo hot, garnished with chopped fresh parsley if desired. Enjoy!

Sheet Pan Fajitas

Ingredients:

- 1 lb (450g) chicken breasts, thinly sliced
- 3 bell peppers (any color), thinly sliced
- 1 large onion, thinly sliced
- 2 tablespoons olive oil
- 2 teaspoons chili powder
- 1 teaspoon ground cumin
- 1 teaspoon paprika
- 1/2 teaspoon garlic powder
- 1/2 teaspoon onion powder
- Salt and black pepper to taste
- 8 small flour tortillas
- Optional toppings: shredded cheese, sour cream, guacamole, salsa, lime wedges, chopped cilantro

Instructions:

Preheat your oven to 400°F (200°C). Line a large baking sheet with parchment paper or aluminum foil for easy cleanup.

In a small bowl, combine the chili powder, cumin, paprika, garlic powder, onion powder, salt, and black pepper.

Place the sliced chicken, bell peppers, and onion on the prepared baking sheet. Drizzle the olive oil over the chicken and vegetables, then sprinkle the seasoning mixture evenly over everything. Toss to coat the chicken and vegetables evenly with the oil and spices.

Spread the chicken and vegetables out in a single layer on the baking sheet. Bake in the preheated oven for 20-25 minutes, or until the chicken is cooked through and the vegetables are tender, stirring halfway through cooking.

While the fajita filling is baking, warm the flour tortillas according to package instructions.

Once the chicken and vegetables are cooked, remove the baking sheet from the oven.

Serve the sheet pan fajitas warm with warm tortillas and your favorite toppings such as shredded cheese, sour cream, guacamole, salsa, lime wedges, and chopped cilantro. Enjoy!

Slow Cooker Chili

Ingredients:

- 1 lb (450g) ground beef or turkey
- 1 onion, diced
- 3 cloves garlic, minced
- 1 bell pepper, diced
- 1 can (14.5 oz) diced tomatoes
- 1 can (15 oz) kidney beans, drained and rinsed
- 1 can (15 oz) black beans, drained and rinsed
- 1 can (6 oz) tomato paste
- 2 cups (480ml) beef or vegetable broth
- 2 tablespoons chili powder
- 1 teaspoon ground cumin
- 1 teaspoon paprika
- 1/2 teaspoon dried oregano
- 1/2 teaspoon salt, or to taste
- 1/4 teaspoon black pepper, or to taste
- Optional toppings: shredded cheese, sour cream, sliced green onions, chopped cilantro, diced avocado

Instructions:

In a large skillet, cook the ground beef or turkey over medium heat until browned. Drain any excess fat.

Transfer the cooked meat to a slow cooker.

Add the diced onion, minced garlic, diced bell pepper, diced tomatoes, kidney beans, black beans, tomato paste, beef or vegetable broth, chili powder, ground cumin, paprika, dried oregano, salt, and black pepper to the slow cooker.

Stir all ingredients in the slow cooker until well combined.

Cover and cook on low heat for 6-8 hours or on high heat for 3-4 hours, stirring occasionally.

Once the chili is cooked and flavors have melded together, taste and adjust seasoning if necessary.

Serve the slow cooker chili hot with your favorite toppings such as shredded cheese, sour cream, sliced green onions, chopped cilantro, and diced avocado. Enjoy!

Easy Beef Stir-Fry

Ingredients:

- 1 lb (450g) beef sirloin or flank steak, thinly sliced
- 2 tablespoons soy sauce
- 1 tablespoon oyster sauce
- 1 tablespoon hoisin sauce
- 1 tablespoon cornstarch
- 2 tablespoons vegetable oil, divided
- 3 cloves garlic, minced
- 1 teaspoon grated ginger
- 1 onion, thinly sliced
- 1 bell pepper, thinly sliced
- 2 cups (180g) broccoli florets
- Salt and black pepper to taste
- Cooked rice or noodles, for serving

Instructions:

In a bowl, combine the thinly sliced beef with soy sauce, oyster sauce, hoisin sauce, and cornstarch. Mix well and let it marinate for about 15-20 minutes.

Heat 1 tablespoon of vegetable oil in a large skillet or wok over medium-high heat.

Add the marinated beef to the skillet and stir-fry for 2-3 minutes until browned. Remove the beef from the skillet and set aside.

In the same skillet, add the remaining tablespoon of vegetable oil.

Add the minced garlic and grated ginger to the skillet and cook for about 30 seconds until fragrant.

Add the sliced onion, bell pepper, and broccoli florets to the skillet. Stir-fry for 3-4 minutes until the vegetables are tender-crisp.

Return the cooked beef to the skillet and stir to combine with the vegetables.

Season with salt and black pepper to taste. Stir-fry for an additional 1-2 minutes to heat everything through.

Serve the easy beef stir-fry hot over cooked rice or noodles. Enjoy!

Veggie-loaded Spaghetti Bolognese

Ingredients:

- 8 oz (225g) spaghetti
- 1 tablespoon olive oil
- 1 onion, diced
- 2 carrots, diced
- 2 celery stalks, diced
- 1 bell pepper, diced
- 3 cloves garlic, minced
- 1 lb (450g) lean ground beef or turkey
- 1 can (14.5 oz) diced tomatoes
- 1 can (6 oz) tomato paste
- 1 cup (240ml) vegetable broth
- 1 teaspoon dried oregano
- 1 teaspoon dried basil
- Salt and black pepper to taste
- Grated Parmesan cheese for serving (optional)
- Chopped fresh parsley for garnish (optional)

Instructions:

Cook the spaghetti according to the package instructions until al dente. Drain and set aside.

In a large skillet or pot, heat the olive oil over medium heat.

Add the diced onion, carrots, celery, and bell pepper to the skillet. Cook, stirring occasionally, for about 5 minutes until the vegetables are softened.

Add the minced garlic to the skillet and cook for an additional 1 minute until fragrant.

Push the vegetables to one side of the skillet and add the ground beef or turkey to the empty side. Cook, breaking up the meat with a spoon, until browned and cooked through.

Stir the cooked meat and vegetables together in the skillet.

Add the diced tomatoes, tomato paste, vegetable broth, dried oregano, and dried basil to the skillet. Stir to combine.

Bring the mixture to a simmer, then reduce the heat to low. Let the sauce simmer gently for about 15-20 minutes, stirring occasionally, to allow the flavors to meld together.

Taste the sauce and season with salt and black pepper as needed.

Serve the veggie-loaded spaghetti Bolognese over cooked spaghetti. Garnish with grated Parmesan cheese and chopped fresh parsley if desired. Enjoy!

Instant Pot Chicken and Rice

Ingredients:

- 1 lb (450g) boneless, skinless chicken breasts, cut into bite-sized pieces
- 1 cup (200g) long-grain white rice
- 1 onion, diced
- 2 cloves garlic, minced
- 1 bell pepper, diced
- 1 carrot, diced
- 1 cup (240ml) chicken broth
- 1 can (14.5 oz) diced tomatoes, undrained
- 1 teaspoon dried thyme
- 1 teaspoon dried oregano
- 1/2 teaspoon paprika
- Salt and black pepper to taste
- Chopped fresh parsley for garnish (optional)

Instructions:

Place the diced chicken breasts, white rice, diced onion, minced garlic, diced bell pepper, and diced carrot in the Instant Pot.
Add the chicken broth and diced tomatoes (with their juices) to the Instant Pot.
Sprinkle the dried thyme, dried oregano, paprika, salt, and black pepper over the ingredients in the Instant Pot.
Stir everything together gently to combine.
Close the Instant Pot lid and set the valve to the sealing position.
Cook on manual (high pressure) mode for 8 minutes.
Once the cooking time is complete, allow the pressure to release naturally for 10 minutes, then carefully do a quick pressure release.
Open the Instant Pot lid and fluff the chicken and rice mixture with a fork.
Taste and adjust seasoning if needed.
Serve the Instant Pot chicken and rice hot, garnished with chopped fresh parsley if desired. Enjoy!

Baked Parmesan Crusted Salmon

Ingredients:

- 4 salmon fillets (about 6 oz each), skinless
- 1/2 cup (50g) grated Parmesan cheese
- 1/4 cup (30g) breadcrumbs
- 2 tablespoons melted butter
- 1 tablespoon chopped fresh parsley
- 1 teaspoon lemon zest
- 1/2 teaspoon garlic powder
- 1/2 teaspoon dried oregano
- Salt and black pepper to taste
- Lemon wedges, for serving
- Chopped fresh parsley, for garnish (optional)

Instructions:

Preheat your oven to 400°F (200°C). Line a baking sheet with parchment paper or lightly grease it with oil to prevent sticking.

In a shallow dish, combine the grated Parmesan cheese, breadcrumbs, melted butter, chopped fresh parsley, lemon zest, garlic powder, dried oregano, salt, and black pepper. Mix well to combine.

Pat the salmon fillets dry with paper towels and season them with a little salt and black pepper.

Dip each salmon fillet into the Parmesan mixture, pressing gently to coat both sides evenly.

Place the coated salmon fillets on the prepared baking sheet.

Bake in the preheated oven for 12-15 minutes, or until the salmon is cooked through and the crust is golden brown and crispy.

Once cooked, remove the salmon from the oven and let it rest for a couple of minutes.

Serve the baked Parmesan crusted salmon hot, garnished with lemon wedges and chopped fresh parsley if desired. Enjoy!

Turkey and Vegetable Skillet

Ingredients:

- 1 lb (450g) ground turkey
- 2 tablespoons olive oil
- 1 onion, diced
- 2 cloves garlic, minced
- 1 bell pepper, diced
- 1 zucchini, diced
- 1 cup (150g) cherry tomatoes, halved
- 2 cups (180g) fresh spinach leaves
- 1 teaspoon dried oregano
- 1 teaspoon dried basil
- Salt and black pepper to taste
- Crushed red pepper flakes (optional)
- Grated Parmesan cheese for serving (optional)

Instructions:

Heat olive oil in a large skillet over medium heat.
Add diced onion and minced garlic to the skillet. Cook, stirring occasionally, for about 2-3 minutes until the onion is translucent and fragrant.
Add ground turkey to the skillet. Cook, breaking it up with a spoon, until browned and cooked through, about 5-7 minutes.
Once the turkey is cooked, add diced bell pepper and zucchini to the skillet. Cook for another 3-4 minutes until the vegetables are slightly tender.
Stir in cherry tomatoes, dried oregano, and dried basil. Cook for an additional 2-3 minutes until the tomatoes start to soften.
Add fresh spinach leaves to the skillet. Cook, stirring occasionally, until the spinach wilts down, about 1-2 minutes.
Season the turkey and vegetable mixture with salt, black pepper, and crushed red pepper flakes if desired. Adjust seasoning according to taste.
Once everything is cooked through and seasoned to your liking, remove the skillet from heat.
Serve the turkey and vegetable skillet hot, optionally topped with grated Parmesan cheese for extra flavor. Enjoy!

Quinoa Stuffed Bell Peppers

Ingredients:

- 4 large bell peppers, any color
- 1 cup (180g) quinoa, rinsed and drained
- 2 cups (480ml) vegetable broth or water
- 1 tablespoon olive oil
- 1 onion, diced
- 2 cloves garlic, minced
- 1 zucchini, diced
- 1 carrot, diced
- 1 cup (150g) cherry tomatoes, halved
- 1 cup (150g) cooked black beans, drained and rinsed
- 1 teaspoon ground cumin
- 1 teaspoon paprika
- Salt and black pepper to taste
- 1/2 cup (60g) grated cheese (such as cheddar or mozzarella), optional
- Chopped fresh parsley or cilantro for garnish (optional)

Instructions:

Preheat your oven to 375°F (190°C). Grease a baking dish large enough to hold the bell peppers.
Cut the tops off the bell peppers and remove the seeds and membranes. Place the hollowed-out bell peppers in the prepared baking dish, cut side up.
In a medium saucepan, combine the quinoa and vegetable broth or water. Bring to a boil, then reduce the heat to low, cover, and simmer for about 15 minutes, or until the quinoa is cooked and the liquid is absorbed.
While the quinoa is cooking, heat olive oil in a large skillet over medium heat. Add diced onion and minced garlic to the skillet. Cook, stirring occasionally, for about 2-3 minutes until the onion is translucent and fragrant.
Add diced zucchini and carrot to the skillet. Cook for another 3-4 minutes until the vegetables are slightly tender.
Stir in cherry tomatoes, cooked black beans, ground cumin, paprika, salt, and black pepper. Cook for an additional 2-3 minutes until the tomatoes start to soften.

Once the quinoa is cooked, add it to the skillet with the vegetable mixture. Stir well to combine all ingredients.

Spoon the quinoa and vegetable mixture into the hollowed-out bell peppers, pressing down gently to pack the filling.

If desired, sprinkle grated cheese over the stuffed bell peppers.

Cover the baking dish with aluminum foil and bake in the preheated oven for 25-30 minutes, or until the bell peppers are tender.

Remove the foil and bake for an additional 5 minutes to melt the cheese and lightly brown the tops of the peppers.

Once cooked, remove the stuffed bell peppers from the oven and let them cool slightly before serving.

Garnish with chopped fresh parsley or cilantro if desired. Serve hot and enjoy!

BBQ Pulled Pork Sandwiches

Ingredients:

- 2 lbs (about 900g) pork shoulder or pork butt
- Salt and black pepper to taste
- 1 tablespoon vegetable oil
- 1 onion, sliced
- 3 cloves garlic, minced
- 1 cup (240ml) BBQ sauce
- 1/2 cup (120ml) chicken broth or water
- 2 tablespoons apple cider vinegar
- 2 tablespoons brown sugar
- 1 tablespoon Worcestershire sauce
- Hamburger buns or sandwich rolls, for serving
- Coleslaw, for topping (optional)

Instructions:

Season the pork shoulder or pork butt generously with salt and black pepper. Heat vegetable oil in a large skillet or Dutch oven over medium-high heat. Add the seasoned pork to the skillet and sear on all sides until browned, about 3-4 minutes per side. Remove the pork from the skillet and set aside.
In the same skillet, add sliced onion and minced garlic. Cook, stirring occasionally, for about 2-3 minutes until the onion is softened and fragrant. Return the seared pork to the skillet with the onion and garlic.
In a small bowl, mix together BBQ sauce, chicken broth or water, apple cider vinegar, brown sugar, and Worcestershire sauce. Pour this mixture over the pork in the skillet.
Cover the skillet with a lid and reduce the heat to low. Let the pork simmer gently for 6-8 hours, or until it is very tender and easily shreds with a fork. Alternatively, you can transfer everything to a slow cooker and cook on low for 8 hours or high for 4 hours.
Once the pork is cooked and tender, remove it from the skillet or slow cooker and shred it using two forks. Return the shredded pork to the skillet or slow cooker and mix it well with the BBQ sauce mixture.
If the sauce is too thin, you can simmer it uncovered over medium heat for a few minutes to thicken it up.

Serve the BBQ pulled pork on hamburger buns or sandwich rolls. Optionally, top with coleslaw for added crunch and flavor. Enjoy your delicious BBQ pulled pork sandwiches!

Creamy Tomato Basil Soup

Ingredients:

- 2 tablespoons olive oil
- 1 onion, chopped
- 3 cloves garlic, minced
- 2 cans (14.5 oz each) diced tomatoes
- 1 can (6 oz) tomato paste
- 4 cups (960ml) vegetable or chicken broth
- 1 cup (240ml) heavy cream
- 1/4 cup (15g) fresh basil leaves, chopped
- 1 teaspoon dried oregano
- 1 teaspoon dried thyme
- Salt and black pepper to taste
- Grated Parmesan cheese for serving (optional)
- Fresh basil leaves for garnish (optional)
- Croutons or breadsticks for serving (optional)

Instructions:

Heat olive oil in a large pot over medium heat.
Add chopped onion to the pot and cook, stirring occasionally, for about 5 minutes until softened and translucent.
Add minced garlic to the pot and cook for an additional 1 minute until fragrant.
Stir in diced tomatoes (with their juices) and tomato paste. Cook for 5 minutes, stirring occasionally.
Add vegetable or chicken broth to the pot and bring the mixture to a simmer.
Once simmering, reduce the heat to low and let the soup cook for about 15-20 minutes to allow the flavors to meld together.
Using an immersion blender or regular blender, puree the soup until smooth.
Return the pureed soup to the pot if using a regular blender.
Stir in heavy cream, chopped fresh basil, dried oregano, and dried thyme. Season with salt and black pepper to taste.
Let the soup simmer for an additional 5 minutes, stirring occasionally.
Taste and adjust seasoning if necessary.
Serve the creamy tomato basil soup hot, garnished with grated Parmesan cheese and fresh basil leaves if desired. Enjoy with croutons or breadsticks on the side, if desired.

Mediterranean Chicken Wraps

Ingredients:

- 1 lb (450g) boneless, skinless chicken breasts, thinly sliced
- 2 tablespoons olive oil
- 2 cloves garlic, minced
- 1 teaspoon dried oregano
- 1 teaspoon dried basil
- Salt and black pepper to taste
- 4 large whole wheat or spinach tortillas
- 1 cup (240g) hummus
- 1 cup (150g) cherry tomatoes, halved
- 1 cucumber, thinly sliced
- 1/2 red onion, thinly sliced
- 1 cup (100g) crumbled feta cheese
- Fresh parsley or cilantro, chopped, for garnish (optional)
- Lemon wedges, for serving

Instructions:

In a bowl, combine the thinly sliced chicken breasts with olive oil, minced garlic, dried oregano, dried basil, salt, and black pepper. Toss to coat the chicken evenly with the seasonings.

Heat a skillet over medium-high heat. Add the seasoned chicken to the skillet and cook for about 5-7 minutes, stirring occasionally, until the chicken is cooked through and browned. Remove from heat and set aside.

Warm the tortillas according to package instructions.

Spread a generous amount of hummus onto each tortilla, leaving a border around the edges.

Divide the cooked chicken evenly among the tortillas, placing it on top of the hummus.

Arrange cherry tomatoes, cucumber slices, and red onion slices on top of the chicken on each tortilla.

Sprinkle crumbled feta cheese over the vegetables.

If desired, garnish with chopped fresh parsley or cilantro.

Squeeze fresh lemon juice over the fillings.

Fold in the sides of each tortilla, then roll up tightly from the bottom to enclose the fillings and form wraps.

Slice the wraps in half diagonally, if desired, and serve immediately. Enjoy your delicious Mediterranean chicken wraps!

Teriyaki Tofu Stir-Fry

Ingredients:

- 14 oz (400g) firm tofu, pressed and cubed
- 2 tablespoons soy sauce
- 2 tablespoons teriyaki sauce
- 1 tablespoon rice vinegar
- 2 tablespoons vegetable oil, divided
- 1 bell pepper, thinly sliced
- 1 carrot, julienned
- 1 cup (150g) broccoli florets
- 1 cup (100g) snap peas
- 3 cloves garlic, minced
- 1 teaspoon grated ginger
- Cooked rice or noodles, for serving
- Sesame seeds and chopped green onions, for garnish (optional)

Instructions:

In a bowl, mix together soy sauce, teriyaki sauce, and rice vinegar.

Add cubed tofu to the sauce mixture and toss gently to coat. Let it marinate for about 10-15 minutes.

Heat 1 tablespoon of vegetable oil in a large skillet or wok over medium-high heat.

Add marinated tofu to the skillet and cook until browned and slightly crispy on all sides, about 5-7 minutes. Remove tofu from the skillet and set aside.

In the same skillet, add the remaining tablespoon of vegetable oil.

Add bell pepper, carrot, broccoli florets, and snap peas to the skillet. Stir-fry for about 3-4 minutes until the vegetables are tender-crisp.

Add minced garlic and grated ginger to the skillet. Stir-fry for an additional 1 minute until fragrant.

Return the cooked tofu to the skillet and pour any remaining marinade over the tofu and vegetables. Stir-fry for another 1-2 minutes until everything is heated through and well combined.

Taste and adjust seasoning if necessary.

Serve the teriyaki tofu stir-fry hot over cooked rice or noodles.

Garnish with sesame seeds and chopped green onions if desired. Enjoy your delicious teriyaki tofu stir-fry!

Sausage and Peppers Pasta

Ingredients:

- 1 pound Italian sausage (sweet or spicy, based on preference)
- 1 onion, thinly sliced
- 2 bell peppers (red, green, or a combination), thinly sliced
- 3 cloves garlic, minced
- 1 can (14.5 ounces) diced tomatoes
- 1 teaspoon dried oregano
- 1/2 teaspoon dried basil
- Salt and pepper to taste
- 1/4 teaspoon red pepper flakes (optional, for added heat)
- 8 ounces pasta (penne, rigatoni, or any shape you prefer)
- Grated Parmesan cheese for serving
- Chopped fresh parsley for garnish (optional)

Instructions:

Cook the Sausage: Heat a large skillet over medium-high heat. Add the Italian sausage links and cook until browned on all sides and cooked through, about 10-12 minutes. Remove from the skillet and let them cool slightly, then slice them into bite-sized pieces.

Prepare the Sauce: In the same skillet, add a little olive oil if needed. Add the sliced onions and bell peppers. Cook, stirring occasionally, until the vegetables are softened, about 5-7 minutes. Add the minced garlic and cook for another minute until fragrant.

Combine Ingredients: Return the sliced sausage to the skillet. Add the diced tomatoes (with their juices), dried oregano, dried basil, salt, pepper, and red pepper flakes (if using). Stir well to combine all the ingredients.

Simmer: Reduce the heat to low and let the sausage and peppers simmer in the tomato sauce for about 10-15 minutes, allowing the flavors to meld together.

Cook the Pasta: While the sauce is simmering, cook the pasta according to the package instructions in a large pot of salted boiling water until al dente. Drain the pasta.

Combine Pasta and Sauce: Add the cooked pasta to the skillet with the sausage and peppers. Toss everything together until the pasta is well coated with the sauce.

Serve: Transfer the sausage and peppers pasta to serving plates or a large serving dish. Sprinkle with grated Parmesan cheese and chopped fresh parsley if desired. Serve hot.

Enjoy your delicious sausage and peppers pasta!

Honey Garlic Shrimp Stir-Fry

Ingredients:

- 1 pound shrimp, peeled and deveined
- 2 tablespoons olive oil or sesame oil
- 4 cloves garlic, minced
- 1 tablespoon ginger, minced
- 1/4 cup honey
- 3 tablespoons soy sauce
- 1 tablespoon rice vinegar
- 1 tablespoon cornstarch
- 1/4 cup water
- Salt and pepper to taste
- Cooked rice or noodles for serving
- Optional garnishes: sliced green onions, sesame seeds, red pepper flakes

Instructions:

Prepare the Sauce: In a small bowl, whisk together the honey, soy sauce, rice vinegar, cornstarch, and water until smooth. Set aside.

Cook the Shrimp: Heat the olive oil or sesame oil in a large skillet or wok over medium-high heat. Add the minced garlic and ginger, and sauté for about 1 minute until fragrant.

Add the Shrimp: Add the shrimp to the skillet in a single layer. Cook for 2-3 minutes on each side until they turn pink and opaque. Season with salt and pepper to taste.

Combine with Sauce: Once the shrimp are cooked, pour the prepared sauce over them in the skillet. Stir well to coat the shrimp in the sauce. Let the sauce simmer for 1-2 minutes until it thickens slightly and coats the shrimp evenly.

Finish and Serve: Remove the skillet from the heat. Serve the honey garlic shrimp over cooked rice or noodles. Garnish with sliced green onions, sesame seeds, and red pepper flakes if desired.

Enjoy: Serve hot and enjoy your delicious honey garlic shrimp stir-fry!

This dish pairs well with steamed vegetables such as broccoli, snow peas, or bell peppers. Feel free to customize the stir-fry with your favorite veggies for added color and flavor.

Cheesy Broccoli and Rice Casserole

Ingredients:

- 2 cups cooked rice (white or brown)
- 2 cups broccoli florets, steamed or blanched
- 1 cup shredded cheddar cheese
- 1/2 cup grated Parmesan cheese
- 1/2 cup sour cream
- 1/2 cup mayonnaise
- 1/2 cup milk
- 2 cloves garlic, minced
- 1 teaspoon onion powder
- Salt and pepper to taste
- 1/2 cup breadcrumbs (optional, for topping)
- 2 tablespoons melted butter (optional, for topping)

Instructions:

Preheat Oven: Preheat your oven to 350°F (175°C). Grease a 9x13-inch baking dish with cooking spray or butter.
Combine Ingredients: In a large mixing bowl, combine the cooked rice, steamed broccoli florets, shredded cheddar cheese, grated Parmesan cheese, sour cream, mayonnaise, milk, minced garlic, onion powder, salt, and pepper. Stir until all ingredients are well combined.
Transfer to Baking Dish: Pour the mixture into the prepared baking dish, spreading it out evenly.
Optional Topping: If desired, mix together the breadcrumbs and melted butter in a small bowl. Sprinkle the breadcrumb mixture evenly over the top of the casserole.
Bake: Place the casserole in the preheated oven and bake for 25-30 minutes, or until the casserole is hot and bubbly, and the top is golden brown.
Serve: Remove the casserole from the oven and let it cool for a few minutes before serving. Serve warm as a delicious side dish or a main course.

Enjoy your cheesy broccoli and rice casserole! Feel free to customize it by adding cooked chicken, ham, or other vegetables to suit your taste.

Greek Salad with Grilled Chicken

Ingredients:

For the Greek Salad:

- 2 boneless, skinless chicken breasts
- 1 tablespoon olive oil
- 1 teaspoon dried oregano
- Salt and pepper to taste
- 1 head of romaine lettuce, chopped
- 1 cucumber, diced
- 1 bell pepper (red, yellow, or green), diced
- 1 cup cherry tomatoes, halved
- 1/2 cup red onion, thinly sliced
- 1/2 cup Kalamata olives, pitted
- 1/2 cup crumbled feta cheese
- Optional: 1/4 cup chopped fresh parsley or mint for garnish

For the Dressing:

- 1/4 cup extra virgin olive oil
- 2 tablespoons red wine vinegar
- 1 teaspoon dried oregano
- 1 clove garlic, minced
- Salt and pepper to taste

Instructions:

Marinate the Chicken: In a bowl, mix together olive oil, dried oregano, salt, and pepper. Add the chicken breasts and coat them evenly with the marinade. Let them marinate for at least 30 minutes, or up to 4 hours in the refrigerator.
Preheat the Grill: Preheat your grill to medium-high heat. Oil the grill grates to prevent sticking.
Grill the Chicken: Remove the chicken breasts from the marinade and discard any excess marinade. Place the chicken breasts on the preheated grill and cook for 6-7 minutes per side, or until they are cooked through and have grill marks. The internal temperature should reach 165°F (74°C). Once cooked, transfer the chicken to a cutting board and let it rest for a few minutes before slicing.

Prepare the Salad: While the chicken is grilling, prepare the salad. In a large salad bowl, combine the chopped romaine lettuce, diced cucumber, diced bell pepper, cherry tomatoes, sliced red onion, and Kalamata olives.

Make the Dressing: In a small bowl, whisk together the extra virgin olive oil, red wine vinegar, dried oregano, minced garlic, salt, and pepper until well combined.

Assemble the Salad: Pour the dressing over the salad and toss until all the ingredients are evenly coated.

Add Grilled Chicken: Slice the grilled chicken breasts into strips. Add them to the salad.

Finish and Serve: Sprinkle the crumbled feta cheese over the salad. Garnish with chopped fresh parsley or mint if desired. Toss gently to combine.

Serve: Serve the Greek salad with grilled chicken immediately as a delicious and healthy meal.

Enjoy your flavorful Greek salad with grilled chicken! It's perfect for a light lunch or dinner.

Beef and Vegetable Kebabs

Ingredients:

For the Marinade:

- 1/4 cup olive oil
- 1/4 cup soy sauce
- 2 tablespoons Worcestershire sauce
- 2 tablespoons balsamic vinegar
- 2 cloves garlic, minced
- 1 teaspoon dried oregano
- 1 teaspoon dried thyme
- Salt and pepper to taste

For the Kebabs:

- 1 pound beef sirloin or tenderloin, cut into 1-inch cubes
- 1 red bell pepper, cut into 1-inch pieces
- 1 green bell pepper, cut into 1-inch pieces
- 1 yellow bell pepper, cut into 1-inch pieces
- 1 red onion, cut into 1-inch pieces
- 8-10 cherry tomatoes
- Optional: mushrooms, zucchini, or other vegetables of your choice

Other:

- Wooden or metal skewers (if using wooden skewers, soak them in water for at least 30 minutes before using to prevent burning)

Instructions:

Prepare the Marinade: In a small bowl, whisk together the olive oil, soy sauce, Worcestershire sauce, balsamic vinegar, minced garlic, dried oregano, dried thyme, salt, and pepper until well combined. Set aside.
Marinate the Beef: Place the beef cubes in a large resealable plastic bag or shallow dish. Pour the marinade over the beef, making sure it's evenly coated. Seal the bag or cover the dish and refrigerate for at least 1 hour, or preferably overnight, to allow the flavors to meld.
Prepare the Vegetables: While the beef is marinating, prepare the vegetables by cutting them into 1-inch pieces.

Assemble the Kebabs: Preheat your grill to medium-high heat. Thread the marinated beef cubes and prepared vegetables onto skewers, alternating between the beef and vegetables.

Grill the Kebabs: Place the assembled kebabs on the preheated grill. Cook for 8-10 minutes, turning occasionally, until the beef is cooked to your desired level of doneness and the vegetables are tender and slightly charred.

Serve: Remove the kebabs from the grill and transfer them to a serving platter. Serve hot, garnished with chopped fresh herbs like parsley or cilantro if desired.

Optional: You can serve the kebabs with rice, couscous, or a fresh salad on the side for a complete meal.

Enjoy your delicious beef and vegetable kebabs! They're perfect for a summer barbecue or a cozy indoor meal.

Lemon Garlic Tilapia

Ingredients:

- 4 tilapia fillets
- 2 tablespoons olive oil
- 2 cloves garlic, minced
- Zest of 1 lemon
- Juice of 1 lemon
- 1 teaspoon dried oregano
- Salt and pepper to taste
- Lemon slices for garnish
- Chopped fresh parsley for garnish

Instructions:

Preheat Oven: Preheat your oven to 400°F (200°C). Line a baking sheet with parchment paper or lightly grease it.
Prepare the Marinade: In a small bowl, whisk together the olive oil, minced garlic, lemon zest, lemon juice, dried oregano, salt, and pepper.
Marinate the Tilapia: Place the tilapia fillets in a shallow dish or a resealable plastic bag. Pour the marinade over the tilapia, making sure each fillet is coated evenly. Allow the fish to marinate for at least 15-20 minutes in the refrigerator.
Bake the Tilapia: Transfer the marinated tilapia fillets to the prepared baking sheet. Pour any remaining marinade over the fish. Arrange lemon slices on top of each fillet. Bake in the preheated oven for 12-15 minutes, or until the fish is cooked through and flakes easily with a fork.
Garnish and Serve: Once cooked, remove the tilapia from the oven. Garnish with chopped fresh parsley and serve immediately.
Optional Grilling: Alternatively, you can grill the tilapia fillets. Preheat your grill to medium-high heat and lightly oil the grill grates. Grill the marinated tilapia fillets for about 4-5 minutes per side, or until they are cooked through and have grill marks.

Serve the lemon garlic tilapia with your favorite side dishes such as steamed vegetables, rice, or a fresh salad. Enjoy your flavorful and aromatic dish!

Vegetarian Black Bean Tacos

Ingredients:

For the Black Beans:

- 1 can (15 ounces) black beans, drained and rinsed
- 1 tablespoon olive oil
- 1 small onion, finely chopped
- 2 cloves garlic, minced
- 1 teaspoon ground cumin
- 1 teaspoon chili powder
- Salt and pepper to taste
- 1/4 cup water (or vegetable broth)

For the Tacos:

- 8 small corn or flour tortillas
- 1 cup shredded lettuce
- 1 cup diced tomatoes
- 1 avocado, sliced
- 1/2 cup shredded cheese (cheddar, Monterey Jack, or Mexican blend)
- 1/4 cup chopped fresh cilantro
- Lime wedges for serving
- Optional toppings: salsa, sour cream, guacamole

Instructions:

Prepare the Black Beans: In a large skillet, heat the olive oil over medium heat. Add the chopped onion and cook until softened, about 3-4 minutes. Add the minced garlic, ground cumin, and chili powder. Cook for an additional 1-2 minutes until fragrant.

Add Black Beans: Add the drained and rinsed black beans to the skillet. Season with salt and pepper to taste. Stir to combine the beans with the onion and spice mixture.

Cook Beans: Pour in the water or vegetable broth to the skillet. Bring the mixture to a simmer and cook for about 5-7 minutes, stirring occasionally, until the beans are heated through and the flavors are well combined. Use a fork or potato masher to lightly mash some of the beans if desired.

Warm Tortillas: While the beans are cooking, warm the tortillas. You can heat them in a dry skillet over medium heat for about 30 seconds on each side or wrap them in foil and warm them in a preheated oven at 350°F (175°C) for 5-10 minutes.

Assemble Tacos: Spoon the black bean mixture onto each warmed tortilla. Top with shredded lettuce, diced tomatoes, sliced avocado, shredded cheese, and chopped cilantro.

Serve: Serve the vegetarian black bean tacos with lime wedges on the side for squeezing over the tacos. Offer additional toppings such as salsa, sour cream, or guacamole if desired.

Enjoy your delicious and flavorful vegetarian black bean tacos! They're perfect for a quick and satisfying weeknight meal.

Pesto Pasta with Cherry Tomatoes

Ingredients:

- 8 ounces (225g) pasta (such as spaghetti, fettuccine, or penne)
- 1 cup cherry tomatoes, halved
- 1/4 cup store-bought or homemade pesto sauce
- 2 tablespoons olive oil
- 2 cloves garlic, minced
- Salt and pepper to taste
- Grated Parmesan cheese for serving
- Fresh basil leaves for garnish (optional)

Instructions:

Cook the Pasta: Bring a large pot of salted water to a boil. Add the pasta and cook according to the package instructions until al dente. Drain the pasta, reserving about 1/2 cup of pasta water, and set aside.

Prepare the Cherry Tomatoes: While the pasta is cooking, halve the cherry tomatoes and set them aside.

Make the Pesto Sauce: If you're using store-bought pesto, you can skip this step. If you're making homemade pesto, combine fresh basil leaves, garlic, pine nuts, Parmesan cheese, and olive oil in a food processor. Pulse until smooth, then season with salt and pepper to taste.

Sauté the Cherry Tomatoes: In a large skillet, heat the olive oil over medium heat. Add the minced garlic and sauté for about 1 minute until fragrant. Add the halved cherry tomatoes to the skillet and cook for 2-3 minutes until they start to soften and release their juices.

Combine Pasta and Pesto: Add the cooked pasta to the skillet with the cherry tomatoes. Spoon the pesto sauce over the pasta and tomatoes. Toss everything together until the pasta is well coated with the pesto sauce and the cherry tomatoes are evenly distributed.

Adjust Consistency: If the pasta seems dry, you can add a splash of reserved pasta water to loosen it up and help the sauce adhere better.

Serve: Transfer the pesto pasta with cherry tomatoes to serving plates or a large serving dish. Sprinkle with grated Parmesan cheese and garnish with fresh basil leaves if desired.

Enjoy: Serve hot and enjoy your delicious pesto pasta with cherry tomatoes as a light and flavorful meal.

This dish is perfect for a quick weeknight dinner or a summer lunch. Feel free to customize it by adding grilled chicken, shrimp, or your favorite vegetables for extra flavor and protein.

Buffalo Chicken Lettuce Wraps

Ingredients:

- 1 pound boneless, skinless chicken breasts, cooked and shredded
- 1/2 cup buffalo sauce (store-bought or homemade)
- 2 tablespoons unsalted butter, melted
- 1 tablespoon honey (optional, for sweetness)
- 1 teaspoon garlic powder
- 1 teaspoon onion powder
- Salt and pepper to taste
- 8 large lettuce leaves (such as iceberg or butter lettuce)
- 1/2 cup diced tomatoes
- 1/4 cup diced red onion
- 1/4 cup crumbled blue cheese or shredded mozzarella cheese (optional)
- Ranch or blue cheese dressing for drizzling (optional)
- Chopped fresh cilantro or parsley for garnish (optional)

Instructions:

Cook and Shred Chicken: Cook the chicken breasts in boiling water or bake them in the oven until fully cooked. Shred the cooked chicken using two forks or by pulsing in a food processor.

Prepare Buffalo Sauce: In a small bowl, mix together the buffalo sauce, melted butter, honey (if using), garlic powder, onion powder, salt, and pepper. Adjust the amount of buffalo sauce according to your desired level of spiciness.

Coat Chicken: Place the shredded chicken in a large skillet or saucepan over medium heat. Pour the buffalo sauce mixture over the chicken and toss to coat evenly. Cook for 2-3 minutes, stirring occasionally, until the chicken is heated through and coated with the sauce.

Assemble Lettuce Wraps: Arrange the lettuce leaves on a serving platter. Spoon the buffalo chicken mixture onto each lettuce leaf.

Add Toppings: Top the buffalo chicken with diced tomatoes, diced red onion, and crumbled blue cheese or shredded mozzarella cheese if desired.

Drizzle Dressing: Drizzle ranch or blue cheese dressing over the buffalo chicken lettuce wraps for extra flavor, if desired.

Garnish: Garnish the lettuce wraps with chopped fresh cilantro or parsley for a pop of color and freshness.

Serve: Serve the buffalo chicken lettuce wraps immediately as a delicious appetizer or light meal.

Enjoy your flavorful and satisfying buffalo chicken lettuce wraps! They're perfect for game days, parties, or a quick weeknight dinner.

Spinach and Ricotta Stuffed Shells

Ingredients:

- 24 jumbo pasta shells
- 2 cups ricotta cheese
- 1 cup grated Parmesan cheese, divided
- 1 cup shredded mozzarella cheese, divided
- 1 large egg, lightly beaten
- 2 cups fresh spinach, chopped
- 2 cloves garlic, minced
- 1 teaspoon dried basil
- 1 teaspoon dried oregano
- Salt and pepper to taste
- 2 cups marinara sauce
- Fresh basil leaves for garnish (optional)

Instructions:

Cook Pasta Shells: Cook the jumbo pasta shells according to the package instructions until al dente. Drain the shells and rinse them under cold water to stop the cooking process. Set aside.

Prepare Filling: In a large mixing bowl, combine the ricotta cheese, 1/2 cup grated Parmesan cheese, 1/2 cup shredded mozzarella cheese, beaten egg, chopped spinach, minced garlic, dried basil, dried oregano, salt, and pepper. Mix well until all ingredients are evenly incorporated.

Stuff Shells: Preheat your oven to 375°F (190°C). Spread a thin layer of marinara sauce on the bottom of a 9x13-inch baking dish. Using a spoon, stuff each cooked pasta shell with the ricotta-spinach mixture and place them in the baking dish.

Top with Sauce and Cheese: Pour the remaining marinara sauce over the stuffed shells, covering them evenly. Sprinkle the remaining grated Parmesan cheese and shredded mozzarella cheese over the top.

Bake: Cover the baking dish with aluminum foil and bake in the preheated oven for 25-30 minutes, or until the cheese is melted and bubbly.

Serve: Once cooked, remove the foil from the baking dish. Garnish the spinach and ricotta stuffed shells with fresh basil leaves if desired. Serve hot and enjoy!

These stuffed shells pair well with a side salad and garlic bread for a complete and satisfying meal. They also make great leftovers for lunch the next day. Enjoy the creamy and cheesy goodness of spinach and ricotta stuffed shells!

Cajun Shrimp and Sausage Skillet

Ingredients:

- 1 pound large shrimp, peeled and deveined
- 12 ounces Andouille sausage, sliced
- 2 tablespoons Cajun seasoning (store-bought or homemade)
- 2 tablespoons olive oil
- 1 onion, diced
- 1 bell pepper (red, green, or yellow), diced
- 3 cloves garlic, minced
- 1 can (14.5 ounces) diced tomatoes, drained
- 1 cup chicken broth
- Salt and pepper to taste
- Cooked rice or crusty bread for serving
- Chopped fresh parsley for garnish (optional)

Instructions:

Season Shrimp and Sausage: In a mixing bowl, toss the peeled and deveined shrimp and sliced Andouille sausage with Cajun seasoning until evenly coated.
Sauté Shrimp and Sausage: Heat olive oil in a large skillet over medium-high heat. Add the seasoned shrimp and sausage to the skillet and cook for 3-4 minutes, stirring occasionally, until the shrimp is pink and cooked through and the sausage is browned. Remove the shrimp and sausage from the skillet and set aside.
Sauté Vegetables: In the same skillet, add diced onion and bell pepper. Cook for 3-4 minutes, stirring occasionally, until the vegetables are softened.
Add Garlic and Tomatoes: Add minced garlic to the skillet and cook for 1 minute until fragrant. Stir in the drained diced tomatoes and cook for an additional 2 minutes.
Deglaze Skillet: Pour chicken broth into the skillet to deglaze, scraping up any browned bits from the bottom of the skillet.
Combine Ingredients: Return the cooked shrimp and sausage to the skillet. Stir everything together and let it simmer for 3-4 minutes to allow the flavors to meld together. Season with salt and pepper to taste.
Serve: Serve the Cajun shrimp and sausage skillet hot over cooked rice or with crusty bread. Garnish with chopped fresh parsley if desired.
Enjoy: Enjoy your flavorful and satisfying Cajun shrimp and sausage skillet!

This dish is perfect for a quick and delicious weeknight dinner. Adjust the level of Cajun seasoning to suit your taste preferences and serve with your favorite side dishes for a complete meal.

Coconut Curry Chicken

Ingredients:

- 1.5 pounds boneless, skinless chicken thighs or breasts, cut into bite-sized pieces
- 2 tablespoons vegetable oil or coconut oil
- 1 onion, finely chopped
- 3 cloves garlic, minced
- 1 tablespoon fresh ginger, grated
- 2 tablespoons curry powder
- 1 teaspoon ground turmeric
- 1 teaspoon ground cumin
- 1 teaspoon ground coriander
- 1 can (14 ounces) coconut milk
- 1 cup chicken broth
- 1 tablespoon soy sauce or fish sauce (optional, for extra flavor)
- 1 tablespoon brown sugar or honey (optional, for sweetness)
- Salt and pepper to taste
- Fresh cilantro leaves for garnish (optional)
- Cooked rice or naan bread for serving

Instructions:

Sauté Aromatics: Heat the vegetable oil or coconut oil in a large skillet or Dutch oven over medium heat. Add the chopped onion and cook until softened, about 3-4 minutes. Add the minced garlic and grated ginger, and cook for an additional 1-2 minutes until fragrant.

Add Spices: Stir in the curry powder, ground turmeric, ground cumin, and ground coriander. Cook for 1 minute, stirring constantly, to toast the spices and release their flavors.

Cook Chicken: Add the bite-sized chicken pieces to the skillet. Cook for 5-6 minutes, stirring occasionally, until the chicken is browned on all sides.

Simmer: Pour in the coconut milk and chicken broth. Add soy sauce or fish sauce (if using) and brown sugar or honey (if using) for extra flavor and sweetness. Stir well to combine all the ingredients.

Simmer: Bring the mixture to a simmer, then reduce the heat to low. Cover and let it simmer gently for 15-20 minutes, stirring occasionally, until the chicken is cooked through and tender. If the sauce becomes too thick, you can add more chicken broth to adjust the consistency.

Season: Taste the curry and adjust the seasoning with salt and pepper as needed.
Serve: Serve the coconut curry chicken hot over cooked rice or with naan bread for dipping. Garnish with fresh cilantro leaves if desired.
Enjoy: Enjoy your delicious coconut curry chicken with its creamy texture and aromatic flavors!

This dish is versatile and can be customized by adding vegetables such as bell peppers, carrots, or potatoes for extra color and nutrition. Feel free to adjust the level of spice to suit your taste preferences.

Caprese Quinoa Salad

Ingredients:

- 1 cup quinoa
- 2 cups water or vegetable broth
- 1 pint cherry tomatoes, halved
- 1 ball fresh mozzarella cheese, diced
- 1/4 cup fresh basil leaves, thinly sliced
- 2 tablespoons extra virgin olive oil
- 1 tablespoon balsamic vinegar
- Salt and pepper to taste
- Optional: Balsamic glaze for drizzling (optional)

Instructions:

Cook Quinoa: Rinse the quinoa under cold water using a fine-mesh sieve to remove any bitterness. In a medium saucepan, bring the water or vegetable broth to a boil. Add the rinsed quinoa, reduce the heat to low, cover, and simmer for 15-20 minutes, or until the quinoa is cooked and the liquid is absorbed. Remove from heat and let it cool slightly.
Prepare Ingredients: While the quinoa is cooking, halve the cherry tomatoes, dice the fresh mozzarella cheese, and thinly slice the fresh basil leaves.
Assemble Salad: In a large mixing bowl, combine the cooked quinoa, halved cherry tomatoes, diced mozzarella cheese, and sliced basil leaves.
Make Dressing: In a small bowl, whisk together the extra virgin olive oil and balsamic vinegar to make the dressing.
Dress Salad: Pour the dressing over the quinoa salad and toss gently to coat all the ingredients evenly. Season with salt and pepper to taste.
Chill: Cover the salad and let it chill in the refrigerator for at least 30 minutes to allow the flavors to meld together.
Serve: Once chilled, serve the Caprese quinoa salad in individual bowls or on a platter. If desired, drizzle with balsamic glaze for extra flavor and presentation.
Enjoy: Enjoy your refreshing and nutritious Caprese quinoa salad as a light and satisfying meal or side dish!

This salad is perfect for picnics, potlucks, or as a healthy lunch option. It's packed with protein, fiber, and vibrant flavors that everyone will love.

Beef and Broccoli Stir-Fry

Ingredients:

- 1 pound flank steak, thinly sliced against the grain
- 3 cups broccoli florets
- 2 tablespoons vegetable oil, divided
- 3 cloves garlic, minced
- 1 teaspoon ginger, minced
- 1/2 cup low-sodium soy sauce
- 1/4 cup water or beef broth
- 2 tablespoons brown sugar
- 1 tablespoon cornstarch
- 1 teaspoon sesame oil
- Cooked rice for serving

Optional Garnishes:

- Sesame seeds
- Sliced green onions
- Red pepper flakes

Instructions:

Marinate the Beef: In a bowl, combine the thinly sliced flank steak with 1 tablespoon of vegetable oil, minced garlic, and minced ginger. Let it marinate for at least 15-30 minutes in the refrigerator.
Prepare the Sauce: In a small bowl, whisk together the low-sodium soy sauce, water or beef broth, brown sugar, cornstarch, and sesame oil until well combined. Set aside.
Cook the Broccoli: Heat the remaining 1 tablespoon of vegetable oil in a large skillet or wok over medium-high heat. Add the broccoli florets and cook for 3-4 minutes, stirring occasionally, until they are bright green and slightly tender. Remove the broccoli from the skillet and set aside.
Stir-Fry the Beef: In the same skillet or wok, add the marinated beef in a single layer. Cook for 2-3 minutes, stirring occasionally, until the beef is browned and cooked through.
Combine Beef and Broccoli: Return the cooked broccoli to the skillet with the beef. Stir to combine.

Add Sauce: Pour the prepared sauce over the beef and broccoli mixture in the skillet. Stir well to coat everything evenly with the sauce.
Simmer: Cook for an additional 2-3 minutes, or until the sauce has thickened and coats the beef and broccoli.
Serve: Serve the beef and broccoli stir-fry hot over cooked rice. Garnish with sesame seeds, sliced green onions, and red pepper flakes if desired.
Enjoy: Enjoy your delicious and flavorful beef and broccoli stir-fry!

Feel free to customize this dish by adding other vegetables such as bell peppers, carrots, or snow peas. You can also adjust the seasoning and sweetness of the sauce according to your taste preferences.

Hawaiian BBQ Chicken Pizza

Ingredients:

- 1 pre-made pizza dough (store-bought or homemade)
- 1 cup barbecue sauce
- 2 cups cooked chicken breast, shredded or diced
- 1 cup pineapple chunks, fresh or canned
- 1 small red onion, thinly sliced
- 2 cups shredded mozzarella cheese
- 1/4 cup chopped fresh cilantro (optional, for garnish)
- Olive oil (for brushing)
- Cornmeal or flour (for dusting)

Instructions:

Preheat Oven: Preheat your oven to the temperature recommended for your pizza dough (usually around 425°F to 450°F or 220°C to 230°C). If you're using a pizza stone, place it in the oven while it preheats.

Prepare Pizza Dough: Roll out the pizza dough on a lightly floured surface to your desired thickness. Transfer the dough to a pizza peel or parchment paper-lined baking sheet that's been dusted with cornmeal or flour.

Brush with Olive Oil: Lightly brush the surface of the pizza dough with olive oil. This will help create a barrier and prevent the crust from becoming soggy from the toppings.

Add BBQ Sauce: Spread barbecue sauce evenly over the oiled pizza dough, leaving a small border around the edges for the crust.

Top with Chicken and Pineapple: Scatter the shredded or diced cooked chicken breast over the barbecue sauce. Distribute the pineapple chunks evenly across the pizza.

Add Red Onion: Sprinkle thinly sliced red onion over the chicken and pineapple.

Add Cheese: Generously sprinkle shredded mozzarella cheese over the entire pizza, covering the toppings evenly.

Bake: Transfer the pizza to the preheated oven and bake for 12-15 minutes, or until the crust is golden brown and the cheese is melted and bubbly.

Garnish and Serve: Remove the pizza from the oven and let it cool for a few minutes. Sprinkle chopped fresh cilantro over the top for a burst of freshness. Slice the pizza and serve hot.

Enjoy: Enjoy your delicious Hawaiian BBQ chicken pizza!

Feel free to customize your pizza by adding other toppings such as cooked bacon, ham, bell peppers, or jalapeños to suit your taste preferences.

Creamy Mushroom Risotto

Ingredients:

- 1 1/2 cups Arborio rice
- 4 cups vegetable or chicken broth
- 2 tablespoons olive oil
- 1 tablespoon butter
- 1 onion, finely chopped
- 2 cloves garlic, minced
- 8 ounces mushrooms (such as cremini or button), sliced
- 1/2 cup dry white wine (optional)
- 1/2 cup grated Parmesan cheese
- Salt and pepper to taste
- Fresh parsley, chopped, for garnish (optional)

Instructions:

Prepare the Broth: In a saucepan, heat the vegetable or chicken broth over medium heat. Once warmed, reduce the heat to low and keep the broth warm throughout the cooking process.

Sauté Mushrooms: In a large skillet or Dutch oven, heat the olive oil and butter over medium heat. Add the chopped onion and sauté for 2-3 minutes until softened. Add the minced garlic and sliced mushrooms, and cook for an additional 5-7 minutes until the mushrooms are browned and tender.

Toast the Rice: Add the Arborio rice to the skillet with the onions and mushrooms. Stir well to coat the rice in the oil and butter mixture. Toast the rice for 1-2 minutes, stirring constantly, until it becomes slightly translucent around the edges.

Deglaze with Wine (Optional): If using dry white wine, pour it into the skillet with the rice and mushrooms. Stir well and cook for 2-3 minutes until the wine is absorbed.

Add Broth: Begin adding the warm broth to the skillet, one ladleful at a time, stirring continuously. Allow each addition of broth to be absorbed by the rice before adding more. Continue this process for about 20-25 minutes, or until the rice is creamy and cooked to your desired consistency. You may not need to use all of the broth.

Finish the Risotto: Once the rice is cooked to your liking, stir in the grated Parmesan cheese until melted and creamy. Season with salt and pepper to taste.

Serve: Remove the skillet from the heat. Garnish the creamy mushroom risotto with chopped fresh parsley, if desired. Serve hot as a delicious main course or side dish.

Enjoy your creamy mushroom risotto, with its rich flavors and creamy texture!

Turkey Meatball Subs

Ingredients:

For the Turkey Meatballs:

- 1 pound ground turkey
- 1/2 cup breadcrumbs
- 1/4 cup grated Parmesan cheese
- 1/4 cup chopped fresh parsley
- 1 egg, beaten
- 2 cloves garlic, minced
- 1 teaspoon dried oregano
- 1 teaspoon dried basil
- Salt and pepper to taste
- Olive oil for cooking

For the Subs:

- 4 to 6 sub rolls or hoagie buns
- 1 cup marinara sauce
- 1 cup shredded mozzarella cheese
- Fresh basil leaves for garnish (optional)

Instructions:

Preheat Oven: Preheat your oven to 375°F (190°C).
Make Turkey Meatballs: In a large mixing bowl, combine ground turkey, breadcrumbs, grated Parmesan cheese, chopped fresh parsley, beaten egg, minced garlic, dried oregano, dried basil, salt, and pepper. Mix until all ingredients are well combined. Shape the mixture into meatballs, about 1 to 1.5 inches in diameter.
Cook Meatballs: Heat olive oil in a large skillet over medium heat. Add the meatballs to the skillet and cook for 6-8 minutes, turning occasionally, until browned on all sides. You may need to cook the meatballs in batches to avoid overcrowding the skillet. Once browned, remove the meatballs from the skillet and set aside.
Assemble Subs: Split the sub rolls or hoagie buns lengthwise, leaving one side attached. Place them on a baking sheet lined with parchment paper or aluminum foil. Spoon marinara sauce onto each roll, then add a few cooked turkey

meatballs on top of the sauce. Sprinkle shredded mozzarella cheese over the meatballs.
Bake: Place the baking sheet in the preheated oven and bake for 10-12 minutes, or until the cheese is melted and bubbly, and the meatballs are heated through.
Garnish and Serve: Remove the turkey meatball subs from the oven. Garnish with fresh basil leaves if desired. Serve hot and enjoy!

These turkey meatball subs are perfect for a quick and hearty meal. Serve them with a side of salad or potato chips for a complete and satisfying lunch or dinner.

Lentil Soup with Spinach

Ingredients:

- 1 cup dried green or brown lentils, rinsed and drained
- 1 tablespoon olive oil
- 1 onion, chopped
- 3 cloves garlic, minced
- 2 carrots, diced
- 2 celery stalks, diced
- 6 cups vegetable or chicken broth
- 1 can (14.5 ounces) diced tomatoes, undrained
- 1 teaspoon dried thyme
- 1 teaspoon dried oregano
- 1/2 teaspoon ground cumin
- Salt and pepper to taste
- 4 cups fresh spinach leaves, chopped
- Juice of 1 lemon (optional)
- Grated Parmesan cheese for serving (optional)
- Crusty bread for serving (optional)

Instructions:

Sauté Aromatics: In a large pot or Dutch oven, heat the olive oil over medium heat. Add the chopped onion and cook for 2-3 minutes until softened. Add the minced garlic and cook for an additional 1 minute until fragrant.
Add Vegetables: Add the diced carrots and celery to the pot. Cook for 5-7 minutes, stirring occasionally, until the vegetables begin to soften.
Add Lentils and Broth: Stir in the rinsed and drained lentils, vegetable or chicken broth, diced tomatoes (undrained), dried thyme, dried oregano, ground cumin, salt, and pepper. Bring the mixture to a boil.
Simmer: Reduce the heat to low, cover the pot, and let the soup simmer for 25-30 minutes, or until the lentils are tender.
Add Spinach: Stir in the chopped fresh spinach leaves and let them wilt in the hot soup for a few minutes.
Adjust Seasoning: Taste the soup and adjust the seasoning with additional salt and pepper if needed. If desired, add a squeeze of fresh lemon juice for brightness.

Serve: Ladle the lentil soup with spinach into bowls. Serve hot, garnished with grated Parmesan cheese if desired, and accompanied by crusty bread for dipping.
Enjoy: Enjoy your hearty and nutritious lentil soup with spinach!

This soup is not only delicious but also versatile. Feel free to customize it by adding other vegetables such as diced potatoes, bell peppers, or zucchini. You can also adjust the consistency by adding more broth if you prefer a thinner soup.

Margherita Flatbread Pizza

Ingredients:

- 2 flatbreads (such as naan or pre-made pizza crust)
- 1 cup marinara sauce
- 2 cups fresh mozzarella cheese, sliced or shredded
- 2 large tomatoes, thinly sliced
- Fresh basil leaves
- Olive oil, for drizzling
- Salt and pepper to taste

Instructions:

Preheat Oven: Preheat your oven to 425°F (220°C). If you have a pizza stone, place it in the oven while preheating.

Prepare Flatbreads: Place the flatbreads on a baking sheet lined with parchment paper or directly on a pizza stone if using one.

Spread Marinara Sauce: Spread marinara sauce evenly over each flatbread, leaving a small border around the edges for the crust.

Add Mozzarella Cheese: Arrange the sliced or shredded mozzarella cheese over the marinara sauce.

Layer Tomatoes: Place the thinly sliced tomatoes over the cheese. Season the tomatoes with salt and pepper to taste.

Bake: Transfer the baking sheet to the preheated oven and bake for 10-12 minutes, or until the cheese is melted and bubbly, and the edges of the flatbread are golden brown.

Garnish with Basil: Remove the flatbreads from the oven and let them cool for a minute. Scatter fresh basil leaves over the top of each pizza.

Drizzle with Olive Oil: Drizzle a little olive oil over the pizzas for added flavor.

Slice and Serve: Use a pizza cutter or sharp knife to slice the Margherita flatbread pizzas into wedges. Serve hot and enjoy!

These Margherita flatbread pizzas are perfect for a quick and easy meal. They're great for lunch, dinner, or as a party appetizer. Feel free to customize them by adding toppings like garlic, olives, or red pepper flakes according to your taste preferences.

Sweet and Sour Tofu

Ingredients:

For the Tofu:

- 1 block (14-16 ounces) extra-firm tofu, pressed and cubed
- 2 tablespoons cornstarch
- Salt and pepper to taste
- 2 tablespoons vegetable oil, for frying

For the Sweet and Sour Sauce:

- 1/4 cup ketchup
- 3 tablespoons rice vinegar
- 2 tablespoons soy sauce
- 2 tablespoons brown sugar
- 1 tablespoon cornstarch
- 1/2 cup pineapple juice (from canned pineapple chunks)
- 1 bell pepper, diced
- 1 onion, diced
- 1 cup pineapple chunks (fresh or canned)

For Garnish (optional):

- Sliced green onions
- Sesame seeds

Instructions:

Prepare the Tofu: Press the tofu to remove excess moisture. Slice the pressed tofu into cubes. In a bowl, toss the tofu cubes with cornstarch until evenly coated. Season with salt and pepper.
Fry the Tofu: Heat vegetable oil in a large skillet or wok over medium-high heat. Add the coated tofu cubes to the skillet in a single layer. Fry for 3-4 minutes on each side, or until golden brown and crispy. Remove the tofu from the skillet and set aside on a plate lined with paper towels to drain excess oil.
Make the Sweet and Sour Sauce: In a small bowl, whisk together the ketchup, rice vinegar, soy sauce, brown sugar, cornstarch, and pineapple juice until smooth.
Cook the Vegetables: In the same skillet or wok, add diced bell pepper and onion. Cook for 2-3 minutes until they start to soften.

Add Sauce: Pour the sweet and sour sauce into the skillet with the cooked vegetables. Stir well and bring to a simmer.

Add Tofu and Pineapple: Return the fried tofu cubes to the skillet with the sauce and vegetables. Add pineapple chunks to the skillet and stir to coat everything in the sauce.

Simmer: Let the tofu and vegetables simmer in the sauce for 2-3 minutes, or until the sauce thickens and coats the tofu and vegetables.

Garnish and Serve: Garnish the sweet and sour tofu with sliced green onions and sesame seeds if desired. Serve hot over cooked rice or noodles.

Enjoy: Enjoy your delicious sweet and sour tofu, packed with sweet, tangy, and savory flavors!

This dish is perfect for a vegetarian meal and can be served as a main course or as part of a larger Asian-inspired spread. Feel free to adjust the sweetness or tanginess of the sauce according to your taste preferences.

Chicken and Vegetable Quesadillas

Ingredients:

- 2 boneless, skinless chicken breasts, cooked and shredded
- 1 red bell pepper, thinly sliced
- 1 green bell pepper, thinly sliced
- 1 small onion, thinly sliced
- 1 cup shredded cheese (such as cheddar or Monterey Jack)
- 4 large flour tortillas
- 2 tablespoons olive oil or vegetable oil
- Salt and pepper to taste
- Optional toppings: salsa, sour cream, guacamole, chopped cilantro

Instructions:

Cook Chicken: Season the chicken breasts with salt and pepper. Cook them in a skillet over medium heat until cooked through, about 6-8 minutes per side. Once cooked, shred the chicken using two forks and set aside.

Prepare Vegetables: In the same skillet, heat 1 tablespoon of olive oil over medium heat. Add the sliced bell peppers and onion to the skillet. Cook for 5-7 minutes, or until the vegetables are softened and slightly caramelized. Season with salt and pepper to taste. Remove from the skillet and set aside.

Assemble Quesadillas: Lay out two tortillas on a clean surface. Divide the shredded chicken, sautéed vegetables, and shredded cheese evenly between the two tortillas. Top each with another tortilla to form two quesadillas.

Cook Quesadillas: Heat the remaining 1 tablespoon of olive oil in a large skillet or griddle over medium heat. Carefully transfer one quesadilla to the skillet and cook for 3-4 minutes on each side, or until the tortillas are golden brown and crispy, and the cheese is melted. Repeat with the second quesadilla.

Slice and Serve: Remove the quesadillas from the skillet and transfer them to a cutting board. Let them cool for a minute, then slice each quesadilla into wedges using a sharp knife or pizza cutter.

Serve: Serve the chicken and vegetable quesadillas hot with your favorite toppings such as salsa, sour cream, guacamole, or chopped cilantro.

Enjoy: Enjoy your delicious and flavorful chicken and vegetable quesadillas as a satisfying meal or snack!

Feel free to customize these quesadillas by adding other vegetables like mushrooms, spinach, or corn, and adjusting the seasoning according to your taste preferences.

Garlic Butter Shrimp Pasta

Ingredients:

- 8 ounces pasta (linguine, spaghetti, or your choice)
- 1 pound large shrimp, peeled and deveined
- 4 tablespoons unsalted butter, divided
- 4 cloves garlic, minced
- 1/4 teaspoon red pepper flakes (optional)
- Salt and black pepper to taste
- 1/4 cup chopped fresh parsley
- 1 tablespoon lemon juice
- Grated Parmesan cheese for serving (optional)

Instructions:

Cook Pasta: Cook the pasta according to the package instructions until al dente. Drain the pasta, reserving 1/2 cup of pasta water, and set aside.
Prepare Shrimp: Pat the shrimp dry with paper towels and season them with salt and black pepper.
Cook Shrimp: In a large skillet, melt 2 tablespoons of butter over medium heat. Add the minced garlic and red pepper flakes (if using), and cook for about 1 minute until fragrant. Add the seasoned shrimp to the skillet and cook for 2-3 minutes per side until they turn pink and opaque. Remove the shrimp from the skillet and set aside.
Make Garlic Butter Sauce: In the same skillet, add the remaining 2 tablespoons of butter and melt it over medium heat. Add the cooked pasta to the skillet along with the chopped parsley and lemon juice. Toss everything together until the pasta is coated evenly with the garlic butter sauce. If the sauce seems too thick, you can add some of the reserved pasta water to loosen it up.
Add Shrimp: Return the cooked shrimp to the skillet with the pasta and gently toss to combine. Cook for another minute to heat the shrimp through.
Serve: Serve the garlic butter shrimp pasta hot, garnished with additional chopped parsley and grated Parmesan cheese if desired.
Enjoy: Enjoy your delicious and flavorful garlic butter shrimp pasta as a satisfying meal!

Feel free to customize this recipe by adding other ingredients like cherry tomatoes, spinach, or mushrooms for extra flavor and nutrition. You can also adjust the amount of garlic, red pepper flakes, and lemon juice according to your taste preferences.

Mediterranean Veggie Bowls

Ingredients:

For the Bowls:

- 2 cups cooked quinoa or couscous
- 1 can (15 ounces) chickpeas, drained and rinsed
- 2 cups cherry tomatoes, halved
- 1 English cucumber, diced
- 1 red bell pepper, diced
- 1/2 red onion, thinly sliced
- 1/2 cup Kalamata olives, pitted
- 1/2 cup crumbled feta cheese
- Fresh parsley or basil leaves for garnish
- Lemon wedges for serving

For the Lemon Herb Dressing:

- 1/4 cup extra virgin olive oil
- 2 tablespoons fresh lemon juice
- 1 clove garlic, minced
- 1 teaspoon dried oregano
- 1 teaspoon dried basil
- Salt and pepper to taste

Instructions:

Prepare the Dressing: In a small bowl, whisk together the extra virgin olive oil, fresh lemon juice, minced garlic, dried oregano, dried basil, salt, and pepper until well combined. Set aside.
Assemble the Bowls: Divide the cooked quinoa or couscous evenly among four serving bowls. Arrange the chickpeas, cherry tomatoes, diced cucumber, diced red bell pepper, thinly sliced red onion, and Kalamata olives on top of the grains.
Add Feta Cheese: Sprinkle crumbled feta cheese over each bowl of vegetables.
Drizzle with Dressing: Drizzle the lemon herb dressing over the Mediterranean veggie bowls, dividing it equally among the bowls.
Garnish: Garnish the bowls with fresh parsley or basil leaves for added flavor and freshness.
Serve: Serve the Mediterranean veggie bowls immediately with lemon wedges on the side for squeezing over the bowls before eating.

Enjoy: Enjoy your flavorful and nutritious Mediterranean veggie bowls as a delicious and satisfying meal!

These veggie bowls are versatile, and you can customize them by adding other Mediterranean-inspired ingredients such as grilled eggplant, roasted red peppers, artichoke hearts, or tzatziki sauce. They are perfect for a healthy lunch or dinner option that's packed with vibrant flavors and colors.

Spicy Sausage and Pepper Pasta

Ingredients:

- 8 ounces pasta (such as penne or rigatoni)
- 1 tablespoon olive oil
- 1 pound spicy Italian sausage, casings removed
- 1 onion, thinly sliced
- 2 bell peppers (red, yellow, or orange), thinly sliced
- 3 cloves garlic, minced
- 1 teaspoon Italian seasoning
- 1/2 teaspoon red pepper flakes (adjust to taste)
- 1 can (14.5 ounces) diced tomatoes
- Salt and black pepper to taste
- 1/4 cup chopped fresh basil or parsley
- Grated Parmesan cheese for serving (optional)

Instructions:

Cook Pasta: Cook the pasta according to the package instructions until al dente. Drain and set aside, reserving 1/2 cup of pasta water.

Cook Sausage: In a large skillet, heat olive oil over medium heat. Add the spicy Italian sausage, breaking it up with a spoon, and cook until browned and cooked through, about 5-7 minutes.

Add Vegetables: Add the sliced onion and bell peppers to the skillet with the sausage. Cook for 5-7 minutes, or until the vegetables are softened.

Add Garlic and Seasonings: Add the minced garlic, Italian seasoning, and red pepper flakes to the skillet. Cook for 1 minute until fragrant.

Add Diced Tomatoes: Pour the diced tomatoes (with their juices) into the skillet. Stir well to combine all the ingredients. Let the mixture simmer for 5-7 minutes to allow the flavors to meld together.

Season: Taste the sauce and season with salt and black pepper as needed.

Combine with Pasta: Add the cooked pasta to the skillet with the sausage and pepper mixture. Toss everything together, adding a splash of reserved pasta water if the sauce seems too thick.

Finish: Stir in the chopped fresh basil or parsley, reserving some for garnish if desired.

Serve: Serve the spicy sausage and pepper pasta hot, garnished with additional fresh herbs and grated Parmesan cheese if desired.

Enjoy: Enjoy your delicious and flavorful spicy sausage and pepper pasta!

Feel free to adjust the level of spiciness by using mild Italian sausage or adding more red pepper flakes according to your taste preferences. You can also add other vegetables such as mushrooms or spinach for extra flavor and nutrition.

Orange Glazed Salmon

Ingredients:

- 4 salmon fillets (about 6 ounces each), skin-on or skinless
- Salt and pepper to taste
- 2 tablespoons olive oil

For the Orange Glaze:

- 1/2 cup orange juice (freshly squeezed if possible)
- Zest of 1 orange
- 2 tablespoons soy sauce
- 2 tablespoons honey or maple syrup
- 2 cloves garlic, minced
- 1 teaspoon grated fresh ginger (optional)
- 1 tablespoon cornstarch (for thickening)
- 1 tablespoon water

Optional Garnish:

- Sesame seeds
- Sliced green onions
- Orange slices

Instructions:

Preheat Oven: Preheat your oven to 400°F (200°C).
Season Salmon: Pat the salmon fillets dry with paper towels and season them with salt and pepper on both sides.
Sear Salmon: Heat olive oil in an oven-safe skillet over medium-high heat. Once the skillet is hot, add the salmon fillets to the skillet, skin-side down if using skin-on fillets. Sear the salmon for 2-3 minutes until the bottom is golden brown.
Make Glaze: In a small bowl, whisk together the orange juice, orange zest, soy sauce, honey or maple syrup, minced garlic, and grated ginger (if using).
Thicken Glaze: In another small bowl, mix together the cornstarch and water to create a slurry. Stir the cornstarch slurry into the orange glaze mixture.
Glaze Salmon: Pour the orange glaze mixture over the seared salmon fillets in the skillet. Move the skillet to the preheated oven.
Bake: Bake the salmon in the oven for 10-12 minutes, or until the salmon is cooked through and flakes easily with a fork.

Broil (Optional): If desired, you can turn on the broiler for the last 1-2 minutes of cooking to caramelize the glaze and give the salmon a slightly charred finish.
Garnish and Serve: Remove the skillet from the oven. Garnish the orange glazed salmon with sesame seeds, sliced green onions, and orange slices if desired.
Serve: Serve the orange glazed salmon hot with your favorite side dishes, such as rice, quinoa, or roasted vegetables.
Enjoy: Enjoy your delicious and flavorful orange glazed salmon!

This dish pairs well with a variety of sides and is perfect for a quick and healthy dinner option.

Ratatouille

Ingredients:

- 1 eggplant, diced
- 2 zucchini, diced
- 1 yellow squash, diced
- 2 bell peppers (red, yellow, or orange), diced
- 1 onion, diced
- 4 cloves garlic, minced
- 2 cups diced tomatoes (fresh or canned)
- 2 tablespoons tomato paste
- 2 tablespoons olive oil
- 1 teaspoon dried thyme
- 1 teaspoon dried oregano
- Salt and pepper to taste
- Fresh basil leaves for garnish (optional)

Instructions:

Prepare Vegetables: Start by dicing all the vegetables into uniform-sized pieces. Keep them separate as they will be added to the pot at different times.
Sauté Onion and Garlic: Heat olive oil in a large pot or Dutch oven over medium heat. Add diced onion and minced garlic to the pot. Sauté for 3-4 minutes until softened and fragrant.
Add Bell Peppers: Add diced bell peppers to the pot with the onions and garlic. Cook for another 3-4 minutes until they start to soften.
Add Eggplant: Add diced eggplant to the pot and cook for 5-6 minutes until it begins to soften.
Add Zucchini and Yellow Squash: Add diced zucchini and yellow squash to the pot. Cook for an additional 4-5 minutes until all the vegetables are tender but not mushy.
Add Tomatoes and Tomato Paste: Stir in diced tomatoes and tomato paste. Mix well to combine all the ingredients.
Season: Season the ratatouille with dried thyme, dried oregano, salt, and pepper to taste. Stir to distribute the seasonings evenly.
Simmer: Reduce the heat to low and let the ratatouille simmer gently for 15-20 minutes, allowing the flavors to meld together and the sauce to thicken slightly.
Adjust Seasoning: Taste and adjust the seasoning if needed.

Garnish and Serve: Garnish the ratatouille with fresh basil leaves just before serving, if desired. Serve hot as a main dish or side dish.
Enjoy: Enjoy your delicious and flavorful ratatouille!

Ratatouille can be served on its own, over cooked grains like rice or quinoa, or alongside crusty bread. It's a versatile dish that can be enjoyed warm or at room temperature.

BBQ Chicken Stuffed Sweet Potatoes

Ingredients:

- 4 medium-sized sweet potatoes
- 2 cups cooked shredded chicken (rotisserie chicken works well)
- 1/2 cup barbecue sauce (plus extra for serving)
- 1/4 cup diced red onion
- 1/4 cup diced bell pepper (any color)
- 1/4 cup shredded cheddar cheese
- Salt and pepper to taste
- Chopped fresh cilantro or green onions for garnish (optional)

Instructions:

Preheat Oven: Preheat your oven to 400°F (200°C).
Prepare Sweet Potatoes: Scrub the sweet potatoes clean and pierce them several times with a fork. Place them on a baking sheet lined with aluminum foil or parchment paper.
Bake Sweet Potatoes: Bake the sweet potatoes in the preheated oven for 45-60 minutes, or until they are tender and easily pierced with a fork.
Prepare BBQ Chicken Mixture: In a mixing bowl, combine the shredded chicken with barbecue sauce, diced red onion, and diced bell pepper. Stir well to coat the chicken evenly with the sauce and vegetables. Season with salt and pepper to taste.
Slice Sweet Potatoes: Once the sweet potatoes are cooked, remove them from the oven and let them cool slightly. Slice each sweet potato lengthwise down the center, being careful not to cut all the way through.
Stuff Sweet Potatoes: Gently fluff the insides of the sweet potatoes with a fork. Stuff each sweet potato with the BBQ chicken mixture, dividing it evenly among them.
Add Cheese: Sprinkle shredded cheddar cheese over the top of each stuffed sweet potato.
Bake Again: Return the stuffed sweet potatoes to the oven and bake for an additional 5-10 minutes, or until the cheese is melted and bubbly.
Garnish and Serve: Remove the stuffed sweet potatoes from the oven. Garnish with chopped fresh cilantro or green onions if desired. Serve hot, with extra barbecue sauce on the side if desired.
Enjoy: Enjoy your delicious and satisfying BBQ chicken stuffed sweet potatoes!

These stuffed sweet potatoes make for a hearty and flavorful meal that's perfect for lunch or dinner. You can customize them by adding additional toppings such as diced avocado, sour cream, or crispy bacon according to your taste preferences.

Veggie Fried Rice

Ingredients:

- 3 cups cooked rice (preferably cold, day-old rice works best)
- 2 tablespoons vegetable oil
- 2 cloves garlic, minced
- 1 small onion, finely chopped
- 2 carrots, diced
- 1 cup frozen peas, thawed
- 1 bell pepper (any color), diced
- 2 eggs, beaten
- 3 tablespoons soy sauce
- 1 tablespoon sesame oil
- Salt and pepper to taste
- Optional: sliced green onions for garnish

Instructions:

Prepare Ingredients: Ensure all vegetables are chopped and ready before you start cooking.

Heat Oil: Heat vegetable oil in a large skillet or wok over medium-high heat.

Sauté Aromatics: Add minced garlic and finely chopped onion to the skillet. Stir-fry for 1-2 minutes until fragrant.

Add Vegetables: Add diced carrots, diced bell pepper, and thawed peas to the skillet. Stir-fry for about 3-4 minutes until the vegetables are tender-crisp.

Push Vegetables Aside: Push the vegetables to one side of the skillet, creating a space to cook the eggs.

Cook Eggs: Pour beaten eggs into the empty space in the skillet. Let them cook undisturbed for a few seconds until they start to set, then scramble them with a spatula until fully cooked.

Combine Ingredients: Once the eggs are cooked, mix them with the vegetables in the skillet.

Add Rice: Add the cooked rice to the skillet. Use a spatula to break up any clumps and mix the rice with the vegetables and eggs.

Season: Drizzle soy sauce and sesame oil over the rice mixture. Season with salt and pepper to taste.

Stir-Fry: Stir-fry everything together for a few minutes until the rice is heated through and evenly coated with the seasonings.

Garnish and Serve: Garnish the veggie fried rice with sliced green onions if desired. Serve hot as a delicious and satisfying meal.

Enjoy: Enjoy your homemade veggie fried rice as a tasty and nutritious dish!

Feel free to customize this recipe by adding other vegetables such as broccoli, mushrooms, or corn. You can also add cooked protein such as tofu, chicken, or shrimp for added flavor and protein.

Creamy Tuscan Chicken

Ingredients:

- 4 boneless, skinless chicken breasts
- Salt and pepper to taste
- 2 tablespoons olive oil
- 4 cloves garlic, minced
- 1 cup chicken broth
- 1 cup heavy cream
- 1/2 cup grated Parmesan cheese
- 1/4 cup sun-dried tomatoes, chopped
- 1 cup baby spinach leaves
- 1 teaspoon dried thyme
- 1 teaspoon dried oregano
- 1 teaspoon dried basil
- Fresh parsley, chopped, for garnish

Instructions:

Prepare Chicken: Season the chicken breasts with salt and pepper on both sides.
Cook Chicken: Heat olive oil in a large skillet over medium-high heat. Add the seasoned chicken breasts to the skillet and cook for 6-7 minutes per side, or until golden brown and cooked through. Remove the chicken from the skillet and set aside.
Make Creamy Sauce: In the same skillet, add minced garlic and cook for 1-2 minutes until fragrant. Pour in chicken broth and scrape up any browned bits from the bottom of the skillet. Let the broth simmer for 2-3 minutes to reduce slightly.
Add Cream and Cheese: Reduce the heat to medium-low. Stir in heavy cream and grated Parmesan cheese until the cheese is melted and the sauce is smooth.
Add Sun-Dried Tomatoes and Herbs: Stir in chopped sun-dried tomatoes, dried thyme, dried oregano, and dried basil.
Add Spinach: Add baby spinach leaves to the skillet and stir until wilted into the sauce.
Return Chicken to Skillet: Return the cooked chicken breasts to the skillet and spoon some of the creamy sauce over the top.
Simmer: Let the chicken simmer in the sauce for 2-3 minutes to heat through and absorb the flavors.

Garnish and Serve: Garnish the creamy Tuscan chicken with chopped fresh parsley before serving.
Enjoy: Serve hot with your favorite side dishes, such as pasta, rice, or crusty bread, and enjoy the creamy and flavorful dish!

This creamy Tuscan chicken is perfect for a special dinner or anytime you're craving a comforting and indulgent meal.

Mexican Street Corn Salad

Ingredients:

- 4 cups cooked corn kernels (from about 4-5 ears of corn)
- 1/4 cup mayonnaise
- 1/4 cup sour cream or Mexican crema
- 1/4 cup finely chopped fresh cilantro
- 1/4 cup crumbled cotija cheese (or feta cheese)
- 1/2 teaspoon chili powder (adjust to taste)
- 1 clove garlic, minced
- 1 jalapeño pepper, seeded and finely chopped (optional)
- 1 lime, juiced
- Salt and pepper to taste
- Additional cotija cheese, chopped cilantro, and lime wedges for garnish

Instructions:

Cook Corn: If using fresh corn, grill or boil the ears of corn until cooked through. Once cooled, carefully cut the kernels off the cobs to yield about 4 cups of cooked corn kernels. Alternatively, you can use canned or frozen corn that has been cooked and drained.

Prepare Dressing: In a large mixing bowl, combine mayonnaise, sour cream (or Mexican crema), minced garlic, chopped cilantro, crumbled cotija cheese, chili powder, and chopped jalapeño pepper (if using). Stir until well combined.

Mix Salad: Add the cooked corn kernels to the dressing mixture. Squeeze fresh lime juice over the corn. Gently toss everything together until the corn is evenly coated with the dressing.

Season: Season the salad with salt and pepper to taste. Adjust the amount of chili powder and lime juice according to your taste preferences.

Chill (Optional): For best flavor, cover the salad and refrigerate for at least 30 minutes to allow the flavors to meld together.

Garnish and Serve: Before serving, garnish the Mexican street corn salad with additional crumbled cotija cheese and chopped cilantro. Serve chilled or at room temperature with lime wedges on the side.

Enjoy: Enjoy your delicious and flavorful Mexican street corn salad as a side dish or appetizer at your next gathering or barbecue!

This salad is bursting with tangy, creamy, and slightly spicy flavors, making it a perfect accompaniment to grilled meats, tacos, or as a standalone dish.

Beef and Mushroom Stroganoff

Ingredients:

- 1 pound beef sirloin steak, thinly sliced (or use beef strips)
- Salt and pepper to taste
- 2 tablespoons olive oil, divided
- 1 onion, finely chopped
- 2 cloves garlic, minced
- 8 ounces mushrooms, sliced (such as cremini or button mushrooms)
- 2 tablespoons all-purpose flour
- 1 cup beef broth
- 1 tablespoon Worcestershire sauce
- 1 tablespoon Dijon mustard
- 1/2 cup sour cream
- 8 ounces egg noodles or pasta of your choice
- Fresh parsley, chopped, for garnish

Instructions:

Cook Noodles: Cook the egg noodles or pasta according to the package instructions until al dente. Drain and set aside.

Prepare Beef: Season the thinly sliced beef with salt and pepper. Heat 1 tablespoon of olive oil in a large skillet over medium-high heat. Add the seasoned beef slices to the skillet and cook for 2-3 minutes per side until browned. Remove the beef from the skillet and set aside.

Sauté Onion, Garlic, and Mushrooms: In the same skillet, add the remaining tablespoon of olive oil. Add finely chopped onion and minced garlic to the skillet. Cook for 2-3 minutes until softened. Add sliced mushrooms to the skillet and cook for an additional 4-5 minutes until the mushrooms are browned and tender.

Make Sauce: Sprinkle 2 tablespoons of all-purpose flour over the mushrooms and onions in the skillet. Stir well to coat the vegetables with the flour. Gradually pour in beef broth while stirring continuously to avoid lumps. Stir in Worcestershire sauce and Dijon mustard.

Simmer: Bring the sauce to a simmer and cook for 2-3 minutes until slightly thickened.

Add Beef and Sour Cream: Return the cooked beef slices to the skillet with the sauce. Stir in sour cream and mix until well combined. Reduce the heat to low and let the stroganoff simmer gently for a few minutes until heated through.

Adjust Seasoning: Taste and adjust the seasoning with salt and pepper if needed.

Serve: Serve the beef and mushroom stroganoff hot over cooked egg noodles or pasta. Garnish with chopped fresh parsley.

Enjoy: Enjoy your delicious and comforting beef and mushroom stroganoff!

This dish is perfect for a cozy weeknight dinner and is sure to be a hit with the whole family. Feel free to customize it by adding other vegetables or using different types of mushrooms according to your preference.

Chickpea Curry

Ingredients:

- 2 tablespoons oil (vegetable or coconut oil works well)
- 1 onion, finely chopped
- 3 cloves garlic, minced
- 1 tablespoon ginger, minced
- 2 teaspoons curry powder
- 1 teaspoon ground cumin
- 1 teaspoon ground coriander
- 1/2 teaspoon turmeric powder
- 1/4 teaspoon cayenne pepper (adjust to taste)
- 1 can (15 ounces) chickpeas, drained and rinsed
- 1 can (14 ounces) diced tomatoes
- 1 can (13.5 ounces) coconut milk
- Salt and pepper to taste
- Fresh cilantro leaves for garnish (optional)
- Cooked rice or naan bread for serving

Instructions:

Sauté Aromatics: Heat oil in a large skillet or pot over medium heat. Add chopped onion and sauté until softened, about 3-4 minutes. Add minced garlic and ginger, and cook for an additional 1-2 minutes until fragrant.

Add Spices: Stir in curry powder, ground cumin, ground coriander, turmeric powder, and cayenne pepper. Cook for about 1 minute to toast the spices and release their flavors.

Add Chickpeas and Tomatoes: Add drained and rinsed chickpeas to the skillet, along with diced tomatoes (with their juices). Stir well to combine all the ingredients.

Simmer: Pour in the coconut milk and stir to combine. Bring the mixture to a simmer, then reduce the heat to low and let it simmer gently for about 10-15 minutes, allowing the flavors to meld together and the sauce to thicken slightly. If the curry becomes too thick, you can add a splash of water or vegetable broth to reach your desired consistency.

Season: Taste the curry and season with salt and pepper as needed, adjusting the seasoning to your preference.

Serve: Serve the chickpea curry hot over cooked rice or with naan bread. Garnish with fresh cilantro leaves if desired.

Enjoy: Enjoy your delicious and flavorful chickpea curry as a satisfying and nutritious meal!

Feel free to customize this recipe by adding other vegetables such as spinach, bell peppers, or cauliflower. You can also adjust the level of spiciness by adding more or less cayenne pepper according to your taste preferences.

Caprese Chicken Skillet

Ingredients:

- 4 boneless, skinless chicken breasts
- Salt and pepper to taste
- 2 tablespoons olive oil
- 2 cloves garlic, minced
- 1 cup cherry tomatoes, halved
- 8 ounces fresh mozzarella cheese, sliced
- Balsamic glaze or reduction, for drizzling
- Fresh basil leaves for garnish

Instructions:

Preheat Oven: Preheat your oven to 375°F (190°C).
Season Chicken: Season the chicken breasts with salt and pepper on both sides.
Sear Chicken: Heat olive oil in an oven-safe skillet over medium-high heat. Once the skillet is hot, add the chicken breasts and sear them for 3-4 minutes on each side until golden brown.
Add Garlic and Tomatoes: Add minced garlic to the skillet with the chicken and cook for 1 minute until fragrant. Add halved cherry tomatoes to the skillet, arranging them around the chicken.
Bake: Transfer the skillet to the preheated oven and bake for 15-20 minutes, or until the chicken is cooked through and reaches an internal temperature of 165°F (74°C).
Add Mozzarella: Remove the skillet from the oven and place slices of fresh mozzarella cheese on top of each chicken breast. Return the skillet to the oven and bake for an additional 3-5 minutes, or until the cheese is melted and bubbly.
Drizzle with Balsamic Glaze: Remove the skillet from the oven. Drizzle balsamic glaze or reduction over the chicken and tomatoes.
Garnish and Serve: Garnish the Caprese chicken skillet with fresh basil leaves.
Enjoy: Serve hot and enjoy your delicious Caprese chicken skillet!

This dish pairs well with a side of cooked pasta, rice, or crusty bread to soak up the flavorful juices. It's a simple yet elegant meal that's perfect for both weeknight dinners and special occasions.

Butternut Squash Soup

Ingredients:

- 1 medium-sized butternut squash (about 2-3 pounds), peeled, seeded, and diced
- 1 tablespoon olive oil
- 1 onion, chopped
- 2 cloves garlic, minced
- 1 carrot, peeled and diced
- 1 celery stalk, diced
- 4 cups vegetable or chicken broth
- 1 teaspoon dried thyme
- 1/2 teaspoon ground cinnamon
- Salt and pepper to taste
- 1/2 cup heavy cream or coconut milk (optional)
- Chopped fresh parsley or chives for garnish (optional)

Instructions:

Preheat Oven: Preheat your oven to 400°F (200°C).
Roast Butternut Squash: Place the diced butternut squash on a baking sheet. Drizzle with olive oil and season with salt and pepper. Toss to coat the squash evenly with oil and seasoning. Roast in the preheated oven for 25-30 minutes, or until the squash is tender and lightly caramelized around the edges.
Sauté Aromatics: While the squash is roasting, heat olive oil in a large pot or Dutch oven over medium heat. Add chopped onion, minced garlic, diced carrot, and diced celery. Sauté for 5-7 minutes, or until the vegetables are softened.
Add Broth and Spices: Pour in the vegetable or chicken broth. Add dried thyme and ground cinnamon. Stir to combine. Bring the mixture to a simmer.
Add Roasted Squash: Once the squash is roasted, add it to the pot with the simmering broth and vegetables. Stir well to combine.
Blend Soup: Using an immersion blender or working in batches with a countertop blender, puree the soup until smooth and creamy.
Adjust Consistency: If the soup is too thick, you can add more broth or water to reach your desired consistency.
Season: Taste the soup and adjust the seasoning with salt and pepper as needed.
Add Cream (Optional): Stir in the heavy cream or coconut milk, if using, to add richness to the soup. Heat through but do not boil.

Serve: Ladle the butternut squash soup into bowls. Garnish with chopped fresh parsley or chives if desired.

Enjoy: Serve hot and enjoy your comforting and flavorful butternut squash soup!

This soup is perfect for warming up on a chilly day and makes a delightful starter or light meal. Pair it with crusty bread or a side salad for a more substantial meal.

Thai Basil Beef Stir-Fry

Ingredients:

- 1 lb (450g) beef sirloin or flank steak, thinly sliced against the grain
- 2 tablespoons vegetable oil
- 4 cloves garlic, minced
- 1-2 Thai bird's eye chilies, finely chopped (adjust to taste)
- 1 bell pepper, thinly sliced
- 1 onion, thinly sliced
- 1 cup fresh basil leaves, loosely packed
- Salt and pepper to taste

For the Sauce:

- 3 tablespoons oyster sauce
- 2 tablespoons soy sauce
- 1 tablespoon fish sauce
- 1 tablespoon brown sugar
- 1 tablespoon water

Optional Garnish:

- Sliced green onions
- Sliced red chili peppers
- Lime wedges

Instructions:

Prepare Sauce: In a small bowl, mix together oyster sauce, soy sauce, fish sauce, brown sugar, and water. Set aside.
Heat Oil: Heat vegetable oil in a large skillet or wok over high heat until shimmering.
Sear Beef: Add the thinly sliced beef to the hot skillet in a single layer. Allow it to sear for about 1-2 minutes without stirring to get a nice brown crust. Flip and cook for another 1-2 minutes until the beef is browned and cooked through. Remove the beef from the skillet and set aside.
Sauté Aromatics: In the same skillet, add minced garlic and chopped Thai bird's eye chilies. Sauté for about 30 seconds until fragrant.
Add Vegetables: Add thinly sliced bell pepper and onion to the skillet. Stir-fry for 2-3 minutes until the vegetables are tender-crisp.

Combine Beef and Sauce: Return the cooked beef to the skillet. Pour the prepared sauce over the beef and vegetables. Stir to coat everything evenly with the sauce.

Add Basil: Add fresh basil leaves to the skillet. Stir-fry for another 1-2 minutes until the basil wilts and the flavors are well combined.

Season: Taste and adjust the seasoning with salt and pepper if needed. Be cautious with salt as the sauces are already salty.

Garnish and Serve: Garnish the Thai basil beef stir-fry with sliced green onions and sliced red chili peppers, if desired. Serve hot over steamed rice or noodles, with lime wedges on the side for squeezing.

Enjoy: Enjoy your flavorful and aromatic Thai basil beef stir-fry!

This dish is quick, easy, and packed with bold Thai flavors. Adjust the level of spiciness by adding more or fewer Thai bird's eye chilies according to your preference.

Spinach and Feta Turkey Burgers

Ingredients:

- 1 pound ground turkey
- 1 cup fresh spinach, chopped
- 1/2 cup crumbled feta cheese
- 1/4 cup finely chopped red onion
- 2 cloves garlic, minced
- 1 tablespoon Worcestershire sauce
- 1 teaspoon dried oregano
- 1/2 teaspoon salt
- 1/4 teaspoon black pepper
- Olive oil or cooking spray for grilling or frying
- Hamburger buns
- Lettuce, tomato, red onion slices (optional, for serving)

Instructions:

Prepare Ingredients: Chop the fresh spinach, crumble the feta cheese, and finely chop the red onion and garlic.

Mix Burger Ingredients: In a large mixing bowl, combine the ground turkey, chopped spinach, crumbled feta cheese, chopped red onion, minced garlic, Worcestershire sauce, dried oregano, salt, and black pepper. Use your hands or a spoon to mix everything together until well combined.

Form Patties: Divide the turkey mixture into 4 equal portions. Shape each portion into a patty, making sure they are evenly sized and compacted to hold their shape.

Cook Patties: Heat a grill or skillet over medium-high heat. Brush the grill grates with olive oil or spray the skillet with cooking spray to prevent sticking. Place the turkey burgers on the grill or skillet and cook for 4-5 minutes per side, or until cooked through and golden brown on the outside. Make sure the internal temperature reaches 165°F (74°C) for safe consumption.

Toast Buns (Optional): If desired, lightly toast the hamburger buns on the grill or skillet for a few minutes until golden.

Assemble Burgers: Place each cooked turkey burger on a hamburger bun. Add lettuce, tomato, and red onion slices if desired.

Serve: Serve the spinach and feta turkey burgers hot, accompanied by your favorite condiments and side dishes.

Enjoy: Enjoy your flavorful and nutritious spinach and feta turkey burgers!

These burgers are packed with flavor and are a healthier alternative to traditional beef burgers. They're perfect for a quick and easy weeknight meal or weekend barbecue.

Lemon Herb Grilled Chicken

Ingredients:

- 4 boneless, skinless chicken breasts
- 2 lemons, juiced
- 3 tablespoons olive oil
- 2 cloves garlic, minced
- 1 tablespoon fresh chopped parsley
- 1 tablespoon fresh chopped thyme
- 1 tablespoon fresh chopped rosemary
- Salt and pepper to taste

Instructions:

Marinate Chicken: In a bowl, whisk together the lemon juice, olive oil, minced garlic, chopped parsley, chopped thyme, and chopped rosemary. Season with salt and pepper to taste. Place the chicken breasts in a shallow dish or resealable plastic bag, and pour the marinade over them. Make sure the chicken is well coated with the marinade. Cover or seal the dish/bag and refrigerate for at least 30 minutes, or up to 4 hours for maximum flavor.
Preheat Grill: Preheat your grill to medium-high heat.
Grill Chicken: Remove the chicken breasts from the marinade and discard any excess marinade. Place the chicken breasts on the preheated grill. Grill for about 6-8 minutes per side, or until the chicken is cooked through and reaches an internal temperature of 165°F (74°C). Cooking time may vary depending on the thickness of the chicken breasts.
Rest Chicken: Once cooked, remove the chicken from the grill and let it rest for a few minutes before serving. This allows the juices to redistribute, resulting in juicier chicken.
Serve: Serve the lemon herb grilled chicken hot, garnished with additional chopped herbs if desired. It pairs well with a variety of side dishes such as grilled vegetables, rice, or a fresh salad.
Enjoy: Enjoy your delicious and flavorful lemon herb grilled chicken!

This recipe is perfect for summer grilling and is sure to be a hit at your next barbecue or outdoor gathering.

www.ingramcontent.com/pod-product-compliance
Lightning Source LLC
LaVergne TN
LVHW081611060526
838201LV00054B/2190